Made in United States
Cleveland, OH
23 May 2025

17185649R10066